THE TENTH MAN

A Miracle of Jewish Faith and Friendship in New Orleans

WRITTEN BY
ARTIE BENNETT

ILLUSTRATED BY
SHIRA NEISS

HOLIDAY HOUSE  NEW YORK

To the survivors, heroes all, and to
Alex Brown, who counted
—A.B.

For Bubby, our faygeleh, who survived with
music and taught us all to sing
—S.N.

Printed and bound in November 2025 at C&C Offset, Shenzhen, China.
The artwork was created with watercolor and digital drawing in Procreate.
www.holidayhouse.com
First Edition
1 3 5 7 9 10 8 6 4 2
ISBN: 978-0-8234-5843-1 (hardcover)

Library of Congress Cataloging-in-Publication Data is available.

EU Authorized Representative: HackettFlynn Ltd, 36 Cloch Choirneal, Balrothery, Co. Dublin, K32 C942, Ireland. EU@walkerpublishinggroup.com

On a steamy Saturday morning in August, the hottest month of the year in New Orleans, nine elderly men gathered for prayer. Their synagogue, Anshe Sfard, once home to a thriving Jewish community, had fallen on hard times.

A young man named Alex Brown had fallen on hard times, too. Heartbroken over his grandfather's passing, he headed toward the murky Mississippi River. On the way, Alex chanced upon an abandoned synagogue.

Something about it seemed familiar. He shrugged it off, though, and resumed his walk. But he stopped in his tracks when he heard faint singing emanating from the shul. *Were these ghosts? The ghosts of Shabbos past?*

Alex shyly knocked on the door. After several moments, an old man, Isak, answered. He looked up at Alex and said, "The tenth man. We've been waiting for the tenth man." Isak led Alex inside as a buzz rippled through the shul.

"The tenth man." "The tenth man."

In Orthodox tradition, one needs ten Jewish men (a minyan) to perform certain prayers, such as Kaddish for the dead. And these men, Holocaust survivors whose world had been destroyed in Eastern Europe, had many people to say Kaddish for. But they didn't have a minyan.

Alex noticed that nearly everyone had a string of numbers tattooed on his forearm.

Isak steered Alex to the front, near the bimah (podium), but Alex made a beeline to the side. *This* was where his grandfather had taken him by the hand so many years ago! And when the men began to sing, it was as if a dam burst inside him. Alex wept and wept.

As the men prayed, Alex noticed two pigeons alight on the nearby window ledge. He knocked on the window, but they wouldn't budge.

Alex wondered if they were his grandfather and grandmother come back, happy to see him return to his roots. (His grandmother's name, Fay, was short for Faiga, which means "bird" in Yiddish.)

Alex went back every Saturday and Sunday (they had Sunday services, too), and he soon became very busy. Having a minyan also allowed them to read from the Torah.

But there had been no one strong enough to remove it from the ark. Alex, however, was a fit young fellow, so he carried the Torah to the bimah, from where it would be read.

His next job would be hagbah, in which the Torah is spread out and hoisted overhead, as high as one can reach, and slowly rotated before the congregation. Isak would perform gelilah, the binding and dressing of the Torah, immediately afterward. They were a team!

Another of Alex's roles was shul secretary. He created files of the many members who had passed on so that the shul could observe their yahrzeit (anniversary of their passing).

"I knew right away that I needed to be there, around those nine men," Alex said. "This was my home."

Over time, Alex developed close friendships with the men. Although he didn't *always* understand their ways. Like when Harry once asked Isak how much he paid for a can of tomatoes at the A&P, and Isak replied, "Fifty-seven cents."

Then Harry revealed that he paid only *fifty* cents at the Winn-Dixie, setting off a round of exaggerated bickering. When Alex asked why they always fought, they simply smiled.

The men even played the occasional practical joke on each other, and soon Alex got into the act. Once Alex tied the tzitzit (fringes) of Isak's tallit (prayer shawl) to the posts of the bimah. When Isak tried to return to his seat, he found himself tethered to the spot.

This made Yossele, someone whom Alex had *never* heard speak, erupt in uncontrollable laughter.

Even *with* Alex, the synagogue sometimes had trouble making a minyan. Alex would then drive to the Jewish assisted-living facility and bundle men into his car—wheelchairs, too—and take them to shul.

Alex wasn't sure if this was kosher, so he suggested that the men say he was family.

When several of the men told security that Alex was their son, the guard seemed perplexed. But he allowed the men to leave. They loved the outing and didn't mind at all being "kidnapped," as Alex later joked.

Because of the hardships the men had suffered in their youth, they tended to be thrifty. Kiddush, a blessing over wine followed by a snack, always came after morning services. Pieces of herring were cut in half, so everybody got a schtickle (a small piece).

And the leftovers were placed back in the jar. Isak showed Alex how to slice a tomato to get the maximum number of slices without it falling apart. It would still be a tomato.

The men were also very resourceful. Once, when the parchment of their Torah separated from the etz chayim, the wooden handles, Joe pulled out a needle and thread and sewed it back together.

They were tailors, shoemakers, grocers, schmatte sellers, deli owners, and ironworkers. They were craftsmen. And they were unlike anybody Alex had ever known.

"Whatever the shul needed, I did. And in return, they gave me life," Alex said.

When antisemitic vandals broke the shul's windows, Alex slept on a cot inside, determined to guard the shul. "I would come to the bimah at midnight as moonlight poured through the stained glass windows. It was stunning," he said.

Although life would eventually take Alex elsewhere, he often went back to visit Anshe Sfard. Sometimes to say farewell.

As a member of the local chevra kadisha, the burial society, Alex knew how to perform taharah, the ritual washing of the deceased.

As word of Alex's new responsibilities reached the shul, the men said to him, "You're gonna wash me," and then smiled.

And when the time came, Alex did. "I said goodbye to all of the men. I was the last person to see them," he said.

When he thinks of his old friends, all gone now, Alex says, "I learned about the Holocaust from them, the heartbreak and sorrow. But even more, they taught me to laugh again. That no matter how bad things were, there was always humor—and there was hope. Though their families had been wiped out, there was something in their souls that could never be extinguished."

Even today, he can hear them saying, "Don't give up. Let's keep going. Let's just keep going."

And so, we must.

In Memoriam

Isak Borenstein • *May 5, 1918–August 18, 2005.*

Isak, a skilled woodworker, designed and built a large wooden menorah for Chabad-Lubavitch of Louisiana. A lighting ceremony is held each Hanukkah, usually at Riverwalk's Spanish Plaza in New Orleans.

Harry "Heschel" Liwerant • *January 5, 1922–April 3, 2005.*

Joseph L. "Yossele" Mexic • *July 3, 1902–August 14, 1999.*

Joseph Sher • *November 27, 1915–March 24, 2016.*

Joe died at the age of 100. He was a tailor, and among his clients were Fats Domino, Al Hirt, and Elvis Presley.

Jack "Jakeleh" Berman • *May 5, 1922–August 21, 2001.*

Jack owned a shop called Jack's Metal Arts and made the gas lamps in the French Quarter.

Henry Galler • *June 14, 1921–October 14, 2012.*

Henry Katz • *January 19, 1922–January 14, 1994.*

Hyman Lader • *July 24, 1906–March 30, 2004.*

Isaac Niederman • *May 6, 1924–January 19, 2015.*

Solomon Radasky • *May 17, 1910–August 4, 2002.*

Ralph Rosenblat • *March 23, 1922–August 22, 2003.*

Nathan Rottersman • *July 18, 1915–June 11, 1996.*

Alex's Grandparents

Benjamin "Benny" Brownstein • *March 9, 1900–December 13, 1988.*

Faiga "Fay" Brownstein • *October 3, 1904–April 17, 1985.*

A Little History

The congregation Agudath Achim Anshe Sfard ("Fraternal Association of Sephardic People"), composed of Hasidic Jews from Lithuania, was established in New Orleans in 1896. (At its founding, the Hasidic movement adopted a distinctive liturgy, Nusach Sfard, derived from that of Sephardic Jews, hence the name Anshe Sfard, even though they weren't Sephardim.) They were a small, itinerant congregation, meeting in people's homes or in rented spaces. By 1900, the congregation was able to purchase a modest building at 1309 South Rampart Street. Growing prosperity and rising membership allowed the congregation to erect their current home, with its impressive barrel-vaulted ceiling, at 2230 Carondelet Street, in the Uptown section of New Orleans. The building was dedicated on September 5, 1926, just in time for High Holiday services.

In 1945, President Truman issued a directive that allowed some Holocaust survivors with sponsorship to relocate to the United States. Then Congress passed the Displaced Persons Act of 1948, allowing for the wider resettlement of European refugees, among whom were many survivors. In the following years, approximately 140,000 Holocaust survivors came to America. They were mainly between twenty and forty years old, for few children and older people survived the horrors.

Most of the refugees settled in the New York area. But some came through ports such as New Orleans to wend their way across this vast land. About 150 stayed on in New Orleans, making their homes here. They were warmly welcomed and supported by the local Jewish community. The survivors faced many obstacles, including learning a new language, and few could imagine the psychological and physical torment they had suffered. But they worked hard and prospered as small businessmen and craftsmen. They built new lives in New Orleans and carved out a close-knit community, becoming each other's surrogate families in place of the families that had perished in Eastern Europe. Calling themselves the New Americans, they founded the New Americans Club in 1961 as an emotional and social support network and to help combat Holocaust denial.

Afterword

Because it was a sweltering summer day, the windows of the shul were open when Alex happened by. Had they been closed—or had the tiny congregation been able to afford air-conditioning—he never would have heard the faint singing and would have continued on his way to the river. "A divine hand led me in that direction," Alex said.

Alex knocked on the shul door, but he could have just entered. After all, it was Shabbat, and he would've been welcome. But Alex had been away from Judaism for a long time. In fact, Alex, at the time, had no idea of the significance of being the tenth man, but he would soon come to understand.

When Alex stumbled upon the shul in 1988, the congregation was composed entirely of Holocaust survivors. They were all born in Poland, from Radom, Łódź, Warsaw, Białystok, and other places. And they were mostly survivors of Auschwitz, but also Mauthausen and Majdanek. (Upon arrival at Auschwitz, inmates given a work assignment had their left forearms tattooed with a distinctive serial number. Those sent directly to the gas chambers were never registered or tattooed.) A short while after one of the survivors passed, an older man who was not a survivor, Henry Katz, joined the shul. He became the gabbai, who keeps everything running smoothly.

One of the men whom Alex ferried to the shul from the assisted-living facility, Woldenberg Village, was Joseph L. "Yossele" Mexic. Born in Odessa, Yossele, who was also not a survivor, quickly became a beloved member of the shul. He had lost a leg when a Mardi Gras float ran over him when he was thirteen.

The survivors, who called themselves "The Greenhorns," all knew and loved Benny, Alex's grandfather (after all, he was a greenhorn, too), and this endeared them to Alex. There was a Jewish corridor on Dryades Street where several of the men had owned shops, but the shops are long gone.

The services had a powerful effect on Alex. "When Harry sang El Malei Rachamim [a Jewish prayer for departed souls], the six million came through in his voice. It came from another place," Alex said.

The synagogue was known as the "Shul for the Stranger," and because you could walk there from downtown New Orleans, guests would occasionally come. Once, when a contingent of Hasidim from Brooklyn were visiting, a terrible thing happened. As Alex was placing the Torah back in the ark, it slipped out and fell. The Hasidim gasped, and the synagogue went silent. "I felt like a failure, like I had cursed the congregation. It was the lowest point of my life," Alex said. When he sat back down, one of the survivors turned to him and said, "Do you have that dollar that you still owe me?" It was a kindly remark, meant to take Alex's mind, momentarily, off his agony. Alex rode around the city that day, unable to do anything else. But the Hasidim convened and decided that neither Alex nor the congregation would have to fast over the incident.

In time, a few other young people joined. One was an Israeli, Gilad "Gil" Landau, who yearned to see America. So he spread out a map, closed his eyes, and pointed. His finger landed smack-dab on New Orleans! There he found work as a pipe welder but longed to connect with the Jewish community. Because Gil read and spoke Hebrew fluently, he was drafted into reading from the Torah.

Gil would remain for a year before moving on to Grambling, in the northern part of the state. A soccer player in Israel, he was given a full scholarship to the historically Black university to be the placekicker for the powerhouse Grambling Tigers football team.

At Grambling, Gil put a mezuzah on the doorpost of his dorm room. But when his teammates, who had never seen such a thing before, would visit, they would press on it, assuming it was a bell. He had to explain what it was. Gil prospered under legendary coach Eddie Robinson, becoming an all-American. And he continued to say the Hebrew prayers alone in his room.

"You never knew who would roll into Anshe Sfard. One day, an itinerant mikvah [ritual bath] salesman wandered in—straight out of *Fiddler on the Roof*—though the shul hadn't had a woman of childbearing age in more than a decade," Alex said.

Anshe Sfard is now run by Chabad, the Lubavitcher Hasidic organization. It's still struggling, but it makes a minyan . . . mostly.

Alex's Backstory

Alex's grandparents Benny and Fay had come to America in the 1920s, escaping the pogroms of their native Ukraine, and settled in Brooklyn, New York. Benny dreamed of becoming a furrier. So he moved the family to New Orleans, where the nutria, a large, beaver-like rodent known for its luxurious fur, had just been introduced. The many fashionable ladies helped make his business a success, despite the city being a subtropical gumbo.

Time passed, and Benny and Fay doted on their grandchildren. Alex's parents weren't religious, so his grandparents sought to bring the warmth and joy of Judaism into their lives. Every Friday night, Grandma Fay made a sumptuous Shabbat dinner for Alex and his cousins.

He loved her cooking and would linger at the candlelit table, polishing off seconds—and then *thirds*—of her fabled chicken. In the morning, Benny would take Alex to synagogue. Alex could point to any page in the siddur—the Jewish prayer book—and Benny would sing the melody in his charming old-world tones. Alex felt like he was wrapped in a cocoon of love.

But sometimes, things change. His cousins moved away. Grandma Fay became too ill to prepare Shabbat dinner. And Benny was now unable to make the walk to synagogue. Alex had changed, too. He was in law school and ashamed of his Eastern European grandparents, with their funny accents and foreign ways.

One day, his grandfather called and asked him to visit. They hadn't seen each other in a long time. Benny, who often sported a red sweater, offered to take Alex to a clothier and buy *him* a red sweater, too. "A red sweater? Why on earth do I need a red sweater?" Alex grumbled. And besides, he was too busy. Alex never came. A few days later, Benny passed away.

It was then that an emptiness began to set in. Alex dropped out of law school. He was racked with remorse over snubbing his grandfather's last attempt to see him. A short while later, Alex would begin his fateful walk to the Mississippi River.

"My grandfather was a larger-than-life character. He was very charismatic. He affected me in death even more than in life," Alex said. "He spoke Yiddish, like them. Benny wanted me to put his shul back together again. This was the only way I could atone for my mistreatment of him."

Alex stayed with the shul for six years, leaving shortly after he met his wife, Margery. They began to attend a Conservative shul, where his uncle Victor taught people how to read Hebrew. "They loved her and she loved them, but she couldn't read Hebrew," he said.

"I had entered the synagogue a broken man. They relit my eternal flame. I owe them everything," Alex said.

Alex's Final Farewell

In 1995, a prominent member of the New Orleans Jewish community asked Alex if he would like to join the local chevra kadisha, the burial society, and Alex accepted without hesitation. He is still an active member of the burial society. "I do taharah to help people, yes. But I do it for myself, too, because every time I do it, it reminds me who I am," Alex said.

Alex visits the cemetery and places pebbles atop the men's gravestones. "These guys were tough. And they toughened me up. They became a part of me, and I became a part of them. I was a hardheaded person. It took something like that to reach me," Alex said. "Judaism is bittersweet," he added. "That's what makes it so beautiful."

The author, Artie Bennett, standing on the steps of Anshe Sfard.

Alex Brown and Artie Bennett.

Interior view of Anshe Sfard.

Glossary

ark: a special cabinet in a synagogue that houses the holy Torah scrolls. It's the holiest place in the synagogue.

Ashkenazim (*OSH-kuh-nah-zum*): a large body of Jews whose ancestors lived in Central and Eastern Europe.

bimah (*BEE-muh*): a raised platform from which the Torah is read.

chevra kadisha (*KHEH-vruh kuh-DEE-shuh*): a group of Jewish people who prepare the deceased for burial. Literally means "holy society."

El Malei Rachamim (*el mah-LAY RAH-khuh-meem*): a Jewish prayer for the soul of a person who has died. Literally means "God, full of compassion."

etz chayim (*ates KHAH-yim*): the wooden poles that the parchment of a Sefer Torah (Torah scroll) is attached to. Literally means "tree of life."

gabbai (*GAA-bie*): a person who assists in the running of a synagogue, including its religious services.

gelilah (*guh-LEE-luh*): the binding and dressing of the Torah scroll after it's been read. This occurs immediately after hagbah.

greenhorn: a newcomer to a country who is unfamiliar with its ways.

hagbah (*HAHG-buh*): the raising and rotating of the Torah scroll before the congregation after it's been read.

Kaddish (*KAH-dish*): a hymn praising God that is recited in every service and chanted as part of the mourning rituals. Literally means "sanctification."

Kiddush (*KIH-dush*): a reception for the congregants after services in which the blessing over wine (also called Kiddush) is recited. Literally means "sanctification."

mezuzah (*muh-ZUH-zuh*): a small piece of parchment containing a biblical passage marked with a Hebrew name of God that is rolled in a case and affixed to the doorpost.

mikvah (*MICK-vuh*): a ritual bath or bathing place for purification.

minyan (*MIN-yun*): a quorum of ten males, age thirteen and up, required by Jewish law for communal worship.

pogrom (*puh-GROM*): the massacre of Jews by local non-Jewish populations, often approved by authorities.

schmatte (*SHMAH-tuh*): a rag or an old, ragged garment.

schtickle (*SHTICK-ul*): a little; a small piece of something.

Sephardim (*suh-FAR-dum*): a large body of Jews whose ancestors lived in Spain, Portugal, and North Africa.

Shabbat (*shuh-BOT*): the Jewish Sabbath, from Friday evening through Saturday night.

Shabbos (*SHAH-bus*): the Ashkenazi pronunciation of the Jewish Sabbath.

shul (*shool*): synagogue.

siddur (*SID-ur*): a Jewish prayer book for everyday use.

taharah (*tuh-HAH-ruh*): the religious ceremony of washing the deceased before burial.

tallit (*TAH-lus*): a shawl with fringed corners worn during prayer.

Torah (*TOR-uh*): a parchment scroll of the first five books of the Hebrew Scriptures, used in synagogue during services.

tzitzit (*TSIH-tsus*): the fringes or tassels worn at the four corners of the tallit.

yahrzeit (*YAR-tsite*): the anniversary of the death of a relative, observed with mourning and the recital of Kaddish.

A Note on Sources

The true story of *The Tenth Man* was collected from multiple Zoom conversations between the author and Alex Brown. The author first got wind of the remarkable tale at the shiva house of his mother-in-law in Michigan, where Alex had come to comfort the bereaved.

https://holocaustsurvivors.org

This website, created by John Menszer, features deeply moving survival stories from Isak Borenstein and Joseph Sher, among others, in their own words.

https://www.isjl.org/encyclopedia-of-southern-jewish-communities.html

The Goldring/Woldenberg Institute of Southern Jewish Life maintains a comprehensive Encyclopedia of Southern Jewish Communities.

https://msje.org/

The Museum of the Southern Jewish Experience, located in New Orleans, is a treasure house of artifacts and information.

https://synagogues-360.anumuseum.org.il/gallery/anshe-sfard

For a panoramic view of the interior of Anshe Sfard.